Not Taking Responsibility

By James Nugent

Forward

We have become a nation of takers. There are more freeloaders than producers. We are by default trying to redistribute the wealth of producers. We should each, take responsibility for ourselves.

Unless we start doing what each of us can do; we will simply bankrupt the entire culture financially and morally, and somebody will take over and tap the one last resource that we will have neglected. The final solution to our problems will be universal slave labor. This will ultimately be the result of our laziness. Of course most of us will be comfortable in our denial until the bitter end.

At first the tiny ruling class will use a pretense of socialism to remedy our social ills. Is free universal health care the start of the decline of the economy? We cannot afford it. We cannot afford a lot of things that would be nice but the answer is not to rob everyone who is producing.

I have a friend who is self-employed. She made a living but medical care was a hit or miss necessity. She eagerly supported Obama Care. Finally the day came when she complied with the mandatory requirement that everybody sign up. To her chagrin it now cost her $4800 a year and the insurance is unusable because her deductible was $5000 a year. She went from middle class, to homeless and a part time worker (producer) in part because could not afford her monthly premiums. Who can afford an extra $400 a month robbed from their personal budget? Her story is repeated millions times all over the United States.

To prevent the above scenario, all people have to do is insist on their right to refuse to pay for other people, and start producing instead of freeloading.

Examples of Freeloading

Why can't people on welfare be required to work or receive job training in critical job fields? Single moms can also receive a subsidy for child care in order to receive job training.

A decade ago I advised a single mom to see if there were any programs for displaced homemakers. There were. She learned to weld. During her union/state apprenticeship she received $22 an hour pay. We she completed the program she became a full union employee. Today she makes $45 an hour. Her other option was to keep on the welfare dole and smoke pot all day. She decided to not be a freeloader.

In my state there are hundreds of different kinds of apprenticeships. There is no excuse for not working. Why not make it a requirement?

I have a friend who was paralyzed from the neck down in a car accident. He eventually recovered and went on the government dole. He was so bored he considered suicide. He spoke with me for 6 hours and we formulated a plan for a productive future.

He organized a plan for community college and employment. He majored in accounting and with adaptive devices he was able to study and attend school. He got perfect grades. Later he attended university and eventually received his Certified Public Accountant designation. Twenty years later he is a full time taxpayer with a small home at the beach and wife and two kids.

His other option was isolation, boredom and death. Almost all physically handicapped people can work and should be required to train and work. Why handicap the disabled by turning them into freeloaders.

I have worked with the mentally disabled. They often stay in public school from age 18 to 21 years, and go to transition to sheltered work programs. Many go on to have productive and happy lives. However, they frequently get turned into free loaders when they find out that they don't have to work if they just sign up the government dole.

Work is good for people and it gives one some dignity.

The other day I had breakfast with two friends. Both women were in transition. One had been unemployed for a year and one will be unemployed next month. As soon as I asked about how the job searches were going, I received a pile of lies and excuses.

Sherri (unemployed for a year) went straight to the lies. She talked about waiting to hear back from a potential employer that already told her no. Her drug history means she can't work there. She also talked about a babysitting job that would pay $20 a week. In all fairness she does occasionally (every other month) make a few dollars babysitting. I dislike lies.

Cathy (about to be unemployed) gave me several excuses for not applying for a new job. The most bizarre was that she had not had time. If I knew when I would be unemployed I would be up all night applying more my next job. In fact I usually have a backup plan and contacts ready to go the minute I hear about upcoming budget problems with my present employer. I read somewhere that the average employee will have at least 8 new jobs in their career because of economic instability. The days of the 40 year employee with one company are extremely rare in today's economy.

Both women did not and will not simply make five applications a day until they get jobs. Both women are freeloaders.

Aren't there any real unemployed people?

There is a shortage of employers. However a real survivor will start their own job. Besides that there are millions of unemployed freeloaders just sitting on their butts and not making five applications for work every day. You see, when you have all day to look for work you should make finding a job your full time job. That's right, you should spend eight hours a day applying for a job! If you don't put in an effort every day you are a freeloader.

Aren't you blaming the victim?

Unemployed people may or may not be at fault for their situation. However once unemployed, how the unemployed person responds is the determining factor in their character. There is no shame in being unemployed. There should be shame in being lazy.

An Explanation not an Excuse

So I do have a modest amount of sympathy for the freeloader. I don't have enough sympathy to support or enable the behavior. For example, I understand that the stress of not have enough money to cover your overhead can make a person sick and unable to work. The cure is to live within your means. I even wrote a short book, on the subject.

It is called "Living within Your Means." No matter what you station in life, one must live responsibly.

Credit Card Debt

Credit card debt is a form of enslavement. People often get in debt trouble because they feel they are entitled to the good things in life. This sense of entitlement is culture wide. Somehow people have been convinced that freeloading is a right. Actually the only things we are entitled to are: life, liberty and pursuit of happiness.

Everybody is entitled to a fair shot. Beyond that you deserve nothing. Gasp! Where is your Christianity?

Christ came to comfort the afflicted. He also came to afflict to comfortable. I give freely and generously to the weak, disenfranchised and the sick. I also will not enable anyone to stay that way. In the New Testament, Acts of the Apostles we are directed to not feed those who will not work. Christianity is not a religion of push overs. Freeloaders constantly forget this point.

So how does one tell who is helpless and hurt and who is lazy? To a certain extent we can never really tell. All we can do is offer aid and comfort and opportunities for the unfortunate person to get on their feet and become independent. If they don't apply for that job or work to their ability, eventually the free handouts must stop.

Years ago my church actually paid hundreds of dollars a month to a freeloader. It took three or four months but eventually the payments stopped. I was outraged but then I realized that occasionally we will be duped by freeloaders. However the risk of being duped is just the cost of being of service to the truly needy.

This all sounds judgmental.

Christians are forbidden to judge each person's final destination in eternity. We are compelled to identify sinful behavior and avoid cooperating with it. Somehow people have twisted this good new into bad news.

Redesigning a life lived irresponsibly.

The freeloader has a basic problem. It is hard to say no to charity when you can get all you need without working. So he/she needs to have some reasons to work. The following reasons may not make sense for you but you can make up your own reasons to work.

1. I want self-respect.
2. I want respect from others.
3. I want freedom choices.
4. I want healthy social relationships.
5. I don't want to be dependent on anyone.
6. I want to develop fully as a human being.
7. I want to be free
8. I ....

The other option is to be a less happy or less functional person.

In order to break the habit of free loading a person must make a fearless survey of everything they do. It is hard work and self-delusion will be rampant. It is probably best to find a professional counselor who can bust you when you are kidding yourself.

If you are married and make life changes your spouse will have to be supportive. Otherwise the relationship is doomed.

What do you really want out of life?

Don't limit yourself by poor choices in the past. Think big and outside the box. Make your life excellent. The big question is what do you need to know and do to achieve your dreams? How can you learn that which you need to know and do?

It actually becomes rewarding to chase after your dreams. It is a joyful experience. It is a healthy lifestyle.

Real People Who Broke Outside the Cage of Freeloading

I have friend who twenty years ago got convicted of drug possession. After abstinence and jail time he became a certified drug counselor and runs his own successful and lucrative drug counseling agency.

I have another friend who left graduate school just because his thesis was rejected. She had never worked a day in her life. She became a failure to launch child. Eventually she decided to make a life for herself. She started his own private school system and was a millionaire by age 35.

Still, another friend lived the life of a prostitute for ten years. She took a break ever now and then in the county jail. She eventually took full advantage of drug rehab and counseling. After accessing Fastweb.com she got the funding for college and graduate school. She now is a consulting Masters level mental health counselor.

The point to these stories is that where there is a will, there is a way. It is not magic. It is just taking responsibility for oneself. We can always start our life over. Just push the reset button and refuse to accept the idea that you are required to be a freeloader.

Consumers vs Producers

To be a healthy and happy person one must be a producer. To let someone else provide for our survival is very attractive but leads to real disability. After laziness becomes a habit, it is hard to break.

During my first week as a counselor, my boss and I visited a welfare mom. As long as she didn't get off her sofa and get a job she was making more money than me. Only when she lost custody of her children (and aid for dependent children) did she start a coffee stand. She blamed me for ruining her life. I hope she has a long a productive life.

A Culture of Freebees

It seems that all you have to do it is promise the general public, something for nothing and you can be president.

During the last election if you voted for Obama you may have received a free I-phone and free health care. In some places they call that a bribe. In America we call it a campaign. We are so corrupt.

It hasn't worked out so well for the winners of that election. They continue disrespect the law and even Congress refuses to work with somebody who promotes culture wide freeloading.

The self-directed Recovery from Freeloading

Before one starts out to live a responsible lifestyle, one must really have a reason to reject freeloading. For myself I like the freedom that comes from independence and the joy of having the resources to share with others.

What do you eat? Where do you sleep? What do you drive and wear? If something or someone pays for these things you are a probably a freeloader.

I know! All of a sudden you sincerely start to prepare defenses (excuses) for why you don't work your way through the world. It doesn't feel good to be caught. Most people choose to enhance their status by lying.

When I worked with homeless people in Shelton Washington most freeloaders had an elaborate and unverifiable story that explained their current status. It usually involved them waiting for an inheritance or being cheated out of money that was rightfully belonged to them. As entertaining as the stories were, they usually neglected to explain why they were not working at the same job as before the potential windfall. If the story included a reason for why they were not working now, it usually involved some alleged insurmountable disabling injury.

My Experience

I have very little empathy for excuses like this, because I was personally injured, at work. I managed to go to work every day, anyway. I went to work even though I was in excruciating pain for almost ten years. For most of a decade I had to carry my brief case in my left hand and shift my stick shift Toyota car with the same hand. My right hand, arm and shoulder were pretty much useless. I never complained and kept up my work load at all costs. I am not saying I was heroic. I was just doing what I could do with what I had to do it. I was not going to be a freeloader.

Over the years I have been plagued with a variety of chronic and acute health conditions. I even had a stroke. Each was issue was dealt with in the same way.

I went to work. When I lost my ability to speak I did two things. First I spent six hours a day teaching myself to speak in three languages again. A language teacher must have perfect speech. Second I started writing more books in case writing became my new profession. I have written fourteen new books in the last eleven months and this is my 35th book in total. My first new book I wrote was a short story about my stroke recovery called "Without Speech."

The final goal is 100 E-books at Amazon.com. Presently I also have 32 paperbacks through Createspace.com and am working in the 19 audio book at Audible.com. The point is that when it looked like I might not be able to teach for a living, I changed my career into being a writer. Eleven months after my stroke I still don't have the endurance to get through the day unless I take one or two naps. I hope to work part time teaching and I will maintain my writing schedule. If all goes well, I will reach my 100 E-book goal within 2 more years.

What's next?

I will always fill my days with meaningful and productive work. I will never be a slacker or a freeloader.

Conclusion

It is easy to be seduced into letting somebody else pay your way through the world. However, really living requires really working and contributing in a meaningful way every day. Anything less is beneath ones dignity. Find your way and never give up.

July 13th 2014

James Nugent

Other Books by James Nugent

How I Sailed From Olympia to the San Juan Islands, and Returned Safely

An Alternative Boating Guide to Southern Puget Sound

How and Why I lived Aboard

Kayaking Budd Inlet in South Puget Sound

Writing E-books and Making the Perfect Book

I Speak Esperanto

The Rainbow Road and Other Signs of God's Love

Living an Abundant Life, Within Your Means

Social Jujitsu and Powerful Principles for Managing Social Conflict

Blackjack on My Small Budget

A Little Benedictine Oblate Manuel

Without Speech

All things work

Loving Time with Your Creator

Personal Adventures in a Life of Learning

The Good News about Being Catholic

E-book Writing and Overcoming Barriers to Creativity

E-book Writing and Organizing Your Ideas

My Forty Days for Life 2013

Lifestyle Reality Observing

How to Sail in the Winter

How to Get Your Kid to Move Out

How to Get What Want

Sex, Abstinence, and Happiness

Cynthia Says Radio Show – Anger is a choice

More Good News about Being Catholic

The Solo Kayak

A Beach Naturalist on Southern Puget Sound

Clean House Clean Life

The Total Catholic Christian

Available at Amazon.com in Kindle E-Book and or Audible Book or Paperback

www.ingramcontent.com/pod-product-compliance
Lightning Source LLC
Chambersburg PA
CBHW071328310526
45789CB00016B/1880